The Cathedral of St Vitus in Prague

IVO HLOBIL

D1712244

◀ The high south tower of the cathedral of St Vitus. Its construction was begun in the 1390s by Peter Parler after his own design, and continued by his sons Wenzel and Johann. The outbreak of the Hussite revolution in 1419 prevented the completion of this the most important work of architecture in the Czech Beautiful Style, to this day the dominant feature of Prague. The tower was not completed until 1562. In 1771 the upper part was modified from a design by the Viennese court architect Niccolo Pacassi, author of the late Baroque remodelling of the Prague Castle. Early in the 20th century the original plans to rebuild the upper part of the tower in Gothic style had to be abandoned due to strong opposition from the architectural heritage lobby.

▲ Sandstone bust of Czech King John of Luxembourg (*1296, son of Count of Luxembourg and Emperor Henry VII and Margaret of Brabant, "John of Bohemia" †1346 at Crécy fighting the English on the side of French King Philip VI). In 1310 the youthful king married Elizabeth (1292–1330), daughter of Czech King Wenceslas II, sister of Wenceslas III, the last Czech king of the Přemyslid dynasty (assassinated in Olomouc in 1306). In 1341 John of Luxembourg donated a tithe of the output of all silver mines in Bohemia for renovation of the tombs of the Czech patrons SS. Wenceslas and Adalbert (Vojtěch) and for the construction of a new cathedral of St Vitus. The bust was carved probably in 1373–75. It is placed with other busts in the wall passage of the inner triforium.

▲ Sandstone bust of Czech King and Holy Roman Emperor Charles IV (*1316, son of John of Luxembourg and Elizabeth Přemyslid, christened Wenceslas, brought up in France where he took the name Charles, margrave of Moravia 1334–36, since 1346 Czech king and later Roman king, since 1355 king of Lombardy, crowned Holy Roman Emperor in Rome in 1355, † in Prague in 1378. Together with his father, Czech king John of Luxembourg, brother John Henry and the newly installed first Prague Archbishop Ernest of Pardubice he laid the foundation stone of the new cathedral of St Vitus, and took great personal interest in the progress of its construction until the end of his life. The bust dates probably from 1373–75.
The upper part of Charles's crown is missing.

Contents

Author of the text

Ivo Hlobil, Institute of Art History, Academy of Sciences of the Czech Republic

Photographers

Ivo Hlobil
Barbara Hucková,
Miroslav Hucek
Jan Kaplan
Jiří Kopřiva
Jana Neubertová
Karel Neubert
Ladislav Neubert
Alexandr Paul
Prokop Paul

Editor Miloš Pokorný

Translators

Till Gottheinerová and Martin Heller

Acknowledgments

Prague Metropolitan Archive (str. 64],
National Gallery in Prague (str. 24]
National Museum (str. 49)

Manufactured by Graspo, a.s. Zlín

Publisher

Opus Publishing Limited
36 Camden Square, London NW1 9XA
E-mail: opuspub@btconnect.com
©1995, 2006 Opus Publishing Limited

Distributor

Karmelitánské nakladatelství, s. r. o.
Kolejní 4, 160 00 Praha 6
Tel. ++ 420 224 316 157
Fax: ++ 420 224 316 160
Mobil: ++420 602 550 108
e-mail: masek@kna.cz
ISBN 0-9535546-2-7

The Construction of the Cathedral

THE METROPOLITAN CATHEDRAL of St Vitus is the most important church in the Czech Lands. Here the kings of Bohemia were crowned and lie buried. It is also the dominating feature of Hradčany and of Old Prague. It stands on the site of two earlier churches of the Prague bishopric (founded in 973) – a pre-Romanesque rotunda built by St Wenceslas, containing the tomb of that first Czech saint (†935), and a Romanesque basilica built by Prince Spytihněv II (1031–61).

The founding of the cathedral fulfilled the long-cherished ambition of the Přemyslids to have the Prague bishopric raised to archbishopric. Their successors, the Luxembourgs, achieved this with the Bull of Pope Clement VI of 30 April 1344. The foundation stone for the cathedral was ceremonially laid on 21 November 1344 by the first Archbishop of Prague, Ernest of Pardubice (1297–1364), King John of Luxembourg and his sons Charles and John. The future King Charles IV (1316–78) initiated and gave decisive support to the construction and the costly furnishing of the new church. Charles became King of Bohemia and in 1355 he was crowned Holy Roman Emperor in Rome. After his marriage in Paris at the age of seven to Blanche de Valois, the prince's name, Wenceslas, had been changed to that of his godfather, King Charles the Fair. The boy was educated at the French court, and one of his tutors was Pierre Roger, the future Pope Clement VI. Charles thus became familiar with the religious symbolism and the political importance of the French cathedrals.

The Prague cathedral is one of the last buildings of its kind. The decision to build in Bohemia a French Gothic cathedral called for immense effort and expenditure. It was part of Charles's endeavour to match the high standard of the countries in Western Europe. Similar aspirations led this Luxembourg monarch, whose mother was Czech, to found Prague University (1348) and to transform Prague into a modern metropolis. Charles had the mighty Karlštejn Castle built so that the imperial Crown Jewels could be venerated in safety.

The first builder of the cathedral (*primus magister*), Matthew of Arras, was summoned to Prague by Charles IV from Avignon. By the time of Matthew's death in 1352 he had built the ground floor of the ambulatory with an array of radiating polygonal chapels, and had raised the piers of the arcades and the walling of the chancel up to the level of the triforium. On the northern side he had reached the sacristy, on the southern side, the Chapel of the Holy Cross. Matthew's design was related to post-classical French Gothic, lightened to the extreme, with a rhythmic pattern of accentuated verticals typical of the late 13th and early 14th centuries, with precedents not only in the south (Toulouse, Narbonne, Rodez) but also in central and northern France (Amiens, Rouen, Troyes).

After Matthew of Arras, the St Vitus lodge was run for a time by an unknown foreman, an acting *magister operis*. In 1356 Charles IV entrusted the continuation of the building programme to the then 23-year-old Peter Parler, who came from a renowned family of builders. Parler brought with him a team of experienced stonemasons, including other talented members of the large Parler family.

Under Peter Parler the St Vitus lodge completed relatively quickly the architecturally remarkable sacristy with two bays – one featuring Matthew's rather elaborate stellar vault, the other Peter's vault of a simpler design – both with suspended bosses (1356–62). Building on the north side of the choir continued with the rectangular chapel of St Sigismund (king of the Burgundians, †524, since 1366 patron saint of Bohemia). In 1367 the Chapel of St Wenceslas – the holiest shrine of the Czech Lands – was consecrated. Charles IV took special interest in it and work on the lavish decorations and furnishing of this chapel continued throughout the next decade. In its vicinity arose the splendid, highly original southern porch (1362–7) of the transept with flying ribs and intricate vaulting. Then work began on the upper part of the façade of the transept. On its eastern side, a seemingly weightless open spiral stairway was added (1371–3) – a masterpiece of Parlerian invention and testament to the skill of his masons. Facing the royal palace, this became the façade until modern times. The entrance was known as the

▲ *Matthew of Arras, first builder of the cathedral (brought to Prague from Avignon by Charles IV in 1344, †1352 in Prague). Portrayed as the* magister operis, *wearing a master's shield. This and other busts on the sides of the inner triforium probably date from 1379–80.*

▲ *Peter Parler, from 1356 the second builder of the cathedral (1333–99), the most important member of a large family of stonemasons–builders; he profoundly influenced the evolution of late Gothic architecture and sculpture.*

Golden Gate, through which, in subsequent generations, passed the coronation and funerary processions of the kings of Bohemia.

From the early 1370s, masons of the St Vitus lodge were building the high choir, supporting it with mighty flying buttresses. A new flamboyant

▲ *The cathedral of St Vitus from the east. The ground floor – the aisles of the presbytery with a wreath of chapels – is the work of Matthew of Arras (before 1352), the high choir with flying buttresses was built by Peter Parler before 1385.*

▶ *The high choir – work of Peter Parler, was completed in 1385. A sombre ground floor contrasts with a luminous triforium and the area of windows. In the foreground the royal mausoleum (1566-89), further back the Neo-Gothic main altar, on the pillars Baroque statues from 1696.*

▲ Stellar vault with a skeletal pendant, east bay of the sacristy. Matthew of Arras and Peter Parler. Begun before 1352, completed after 1356.

▲ A simpler stellar vault with a skeletal pendant, west bay of the sacristy – Peter Parler. After 1356.

▲ Stellar domical vault of the chapel of St Wenceslas. Peter Parler, 1366. The ribs form an eight-pointed star with a cross in the centre.

▲ Alternating spiral open staircase, south-eastern pillar of the transept – Peter Parler, 1372. An original, much admired feature of the cathedral. The reliefs of the arms of Czech crown lands were painted by Master Oswald and his assistants.

▲ Jumping vault with a skeletal rib conoid, Golden Gate (Porta aurea), Peter Parler, 1368. Detail of the sophisticated structure and architectural decoration of the ceremonial entrance to the cathedral.

▲ Net vault, high choir – Peter Parler, 1385. The breaks between bays are disguised in the interest of creating an impression of a continuous space. It was the first vault of its kind, later often imitated.

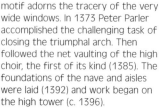

motif adorns the tracery of the very wide windows. In 1373 Peter Parler accomplished the challenging task of closing the triumphal arch. Then followed the net vaulting of the high choir, the first of its kind (1385). The foundations of the nave and aisles were laid (1392) and work began on the high tower (c. 1396).

The two earliest builders differed considerably in their approach to the design of St Vitus's Cathedral.

Matthew of Arras introduced post-classical French architecture to Prague; Peter Parler created a work that represented the final phase of Late Gothic architecture in the German-speaking countries of Central Europe. Parler strove for original solutions, giving individual character to architectural elements and spaces by creating intricate vaulting hitherto unseen, except in England, using flamboyant tracery, diversity of detailing and returning to the full

forms of High Gothic. Prague cathedral thus gained from the architectural and symbolic contrast of Matthew's sombre ground floor and Parler's high, brighly lit chancel.

As *magister operis*, Peter Parler was in charge of the St Vitus lodge almost to the end of his life (1399). He settled in Prague, and became a respected town councillor. He built a new stone bridge across the Vltava (Charles Bridge), the chapel of All Saints in the palace at Prague Castle,

▲ Ernest of Pardubice, first archbishop of Prague (†1364) – trusted adviser and friend of Charles IV, chancellor of the university founded in 1348.

▲ Canon Nicholas Holubec, second director of works (†1355). The bust's expressiveness contrasts with the serenity characteristic of the others.

▲ Beneš Krabice of Weitmile, third director of works (†1375) keeper of the rare surviving early accounts of Peter Parler's St Vitus lodge.

▲ John of Jenštejn, third archbishop of Prague, resigned in 1396 due to his conflict with king Wenceslas IV, †1400 in Rome. His secretary John of Nepomuk died under torture in 1393; his body was thrown into the river.

▲ Clerk (notarius) Andrew Kotlik (canon of St Vitus chapter, †1380), later became the fourth director of works of the cathedral. He wrote, in Latin, the other surviving accounts of the lodge under Peter Parler.

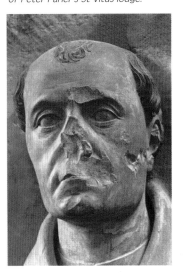

▲ Wenceslas of Radeč, fifth director of works, (canon 1379–1417) – the only bust carved from Prague slate, it is considered to be one of the masterpieces of the Czech Beautiful Style. Carved after 1385.

and a choir in the Church of St Bartholomew at Kolin nad Labem. He probably laid also the foundations of St Barbara's at Kutná Hora.

His position was taken over by his sons, both former stonemasons in the lodge: first Wenzel and then Johann (1398–1406), followed by Petrlik, probably their kinsman. Under their direction, the high tower was raised and a lancet arch was erected at the southern end of the transept.

In 1419 work on the cathedral ceased for a long period – an untimely end to the Luxembourg phase of construction.

In the course of the subsequent Hussite revolution the rich furnishing and decorations were repeatedly plundered or vandalised.
First, the German king Sigismund, not acknowledged in Bohemia, occupied Prague Castle and had himself crowned in St Vitus's on 28 July 1420, paying the mercenaries of the

Crusaders' army in silver and gold from the reliquaries of the cathedral treasure that he confiscated.

On 10 June 1421 the cathedral was plundered by the radical Hussites, inflamed by their hatred of pictures and any show of opulence. It was only thanks to the intervention of Prague's maltsters and other more thoughtful citizens that a complete destruction of Prague Castle was averted at that time.

The Golden Gate and the mosaic of the Last Judgment

In 1367 the three-arched Golden Gate and porch of the portal at the southern end of the transept became the ceremonial entrance to the new cathedral and to the Chapel of St Wenceslas. A sacristy above the gate served as repository for the chapel's precious relics; to be later converted into the Crown Chamber.

The task of providing the statuary for the Golden Gate gave Peter Parler and his stonemasons their first chance to apply their skill on a large scale. In the tabernacle of the central pillar of the portal probably stood a statue of the Virgin Mary, flanked by Charles IV, Empress Elizabeth of Pomorze (Pomerania) and others in adoration. This group was extended by statues of the twelve Apostles. The remaining sculptures, a pelican and a phoenix, can be seen below the vault opposite.

On return in 1369 from his progress in Italy for the coronation of his wife Charles commissioned for the façade of the Golden Gate a large mosaic depicting the Last Judgment, a work without equal north of the Alps. In the centre, in a *mandorla*, is Christ the Judge, with the six Czech patron saints beneath. Charles IV and Elizabeth of Pomorze kneel in the spandrels. The scenes to Christ's right and left show the saved and the lost;

◀ *Emperor Charles IV, donor of the mosaic, kneeling with his wife Elizabeth of Pomorze (Pomerania) below the Last Judgment wearing the imperial crown of Roman kings over a mitre.*

▲ The Last Judgment, mosaic above the Golden Gate – made in 1370–71 by Venetian mosaicists with local assistants, possibly from a cartoon by Nicoletto Semitecolo, a Venetian painter, certainly in accordance with the Emperor's concept. In 1992–2001 the mosaic was expertly restored by the Getty Conservation Institute.

Above left St Peter, St John and four other apostles. To their right, Virgin Mary kneeling in prayer. Below, angels helping the resurrected rise from their graves; Christ the Judge, surrounded by an aureole and angels, below the land patrons, and in the spandrels the donor and Empress Elizabeth of Pomorze (Pomerania).

▲ Detail – Veraikon (vera icon) – this imaginative addition above the centre of the mosaic of the Last Judgment reproduces the miraculous impression of the face of suffering Jesus made on a napkin that according to legend St Veronica kindly offered him to wipe his brow on the sorrowful way to Golgotha.

◄ *Central part of the mosaic of the Last Judgment. Christ the Judge – the wounds of crucifixion visible in his right side, on feet and hands – condemning the sinners with his left hand, surrounded with rays of light and a rainbow – symbol of hope. The mandorla is carried by angels with the tools of his Passion – Arma Christi. The land patrons intercede for the Czech kingdom – on the right St Wenceslas, St Ludmila, St Adalbert (Vojtěch), to the left St Vitus, St Sigismund, St Procopius.*
▶ *Detail – head of an Apostle.*
▼ *Detail – medieval notion of hell.*

above them is the Virgin interceding, with John the Baptist and the Apostles. Above Christ is the Veraikon. A copy of the Roman Veraikon, which Charles brought from Italy, has been preserved in the cathedral treasure. The mosaic is the work of Venetian artisans, its composition distantly related to Giotto's *Last Judgment* in the Scrovegni chapel in Padua, but including clear evidence of Czech creative tradition. The original colouring of the mosaic was recently restored with the cooperation of the Getty Conservation Institute and the University of California.

The Coronation Jewels

Once the insignia of the sovereign Bohemian monarchs, today the Crown Jewels are symbols of the royal past of the Czech state. They are kept under seven locks in the Crown Chamber, the one-time sacristy of the Chapel of St Wenceslas, adapted for the purpose in the late 19th century. They are put on display only on rare occasions, such as the proclamation of the Czech Republic on 10 January 1993.

The oldest jewel is the St Wenceslas Crown, made for the coronation of Charles IV as king of Bohemia and of Blanche de Valois as queen in Prague on 2 September 1347. Previous to this, Charles donated the crown to St Wenceslas. At the King's request, Pope Clement VI issued a special Bull for its protection, with the threat of excommunication to anyone who might dare "appropriate or desecrate it, or pawn it".

The St Wenceslas Crown was in the custody of the St Vitus Chapter, which was entitled to a fee of 200 talents of silver on the occasion of each coronation. The design of the crown, with four large *fleurs-de-lis* on the headband, closed by two inter-secting arches, was based on the royal insignia of the last Přemyslids. It was also influenced by the symbolism of the crowns of the kings of France as shown by the addition on top of the crown of a reliquary cross with a

◀ The St Wenceslas Crown, symbol of the royal past and sovereignty of the Czech state, diameter and height 19 cm, gold (21-22 carat), 96 gemstones – blue sapphires, red spinels, in the centre of the frontal fleur-de-lis a large ruby (rubellite, according to a recent analysis), emeralds, 20 pearls topped by a cross with an engraved sapphire covering a particle from Christ's Crown of Thorns , weight 2358.3 g. Made in 1347, altered before 1378. Behind the crown is its original painted leather case with heraldic symbols.
◀ The Royal Orb – h. 22 cm, gold (18 carat). On the hemispheres wrought reliefs with scenes from the Genesis and the life of King David, surmounted by a cross adorned with gemstones, enamel ornaments and pearls, with six sphinxes at its foot.
◀ The Royal Sceptre – l. 67 cm, gold (18 carat), with a large spinel on top (2.5 x 1.75 cm). Mounted on the flourish are 4 spinels, 4 sapphires and pearls. Weight 1013 g. The orb and sceptre were made in the Low Countries in the 1640s as imperial insignia.

thorn from Christ's Crown of Thorns, kept since the reign of Saint Louis in the Sainte-Chapelle in Paris . The arches of the St Wenceslas Crown are embellished with links of a jewelled golden belt with cabochon gemstones and pearls in settings, a gift to Blanche de Valois from King Charles the Fair on the occasion of her wedding in Paris with Charles IV in 1324. The present number and arrangement of the gems are the result of a final adaptation carried out in the last years of Charles's life. The most valuable gems adorn the front of the crown. Its strong visual impact is due to the interaction of polished gold and the projecting gemstones, especially the red spinels and blue sapphires. The crown is kept in its original round case of painted leather made in 1347, with the arms of Charles IV – the imperial eagle and the Czech lion – at the top.

The gold Coronation Cross came to

▲ The golden Coronation Cross. Charles IV placed in it the most precious relics of the Middle Ages – fragments of the Holy Rood, two particles of Christ's Crown of Thorns donated in 1356 by King John II the Good of France, and other relics. It is adorned with nine cameos of Roman and Byzantine origin, 20 sapphires, 1 emerald, 2 spinels, 24 pearls and crystal plates. H. 62.5 cm, w. 41.5 cm. After 1354.
The Early Renaissance foot was donated c. 1526 by Ladislav Jagiello, king of Bohemia and Hungary.

the cathedral later from Karlštejn Castle. Czech regalia include the St Wenceslas Sword, first mentioned in 1333.

The Royal Orb and Sceptre, dating from the Renaissance, were originally part of the imperial coronation insignia of the Habsburgs, kings of Bohemia from 1526.

The Chapel of St Wenceslas

The Chapel of St Wenceslas is a separate, extraordinary shrine in the cathedral. The tomb of St Wenceslas, the most hallowed in the Czech Lands, has stood on this site since the saint's body was brought from the town of Boleslav to the southern apse of the St Vitus rotunda by the repentant fratricide Boleslav I (c. 915–73).

In the Middle Ages, worship of St Wenceslas reached its apogee under Charles IV. The tithes from Bohemia's gold and silver mines, dedicated to the building of the cathedral, were primarily assigned for the embellishment of the tombs of the patron saints of the land, St Wenceslas and St Adalbert. The interior of the Chapel of St Wenceslas, consecrated in 1367 in the emperor's presence, is an enclosed,

▲ *Pastoforium – tabernacle for the Blessed Sacrament from gilded wrought iron, h. 210 cm. Made in 1373–75 by Master Wenceslas, blacksmith of the St Vitus lodge, probably from Peter Parler's design.*
▲ *The bronze knocker in the form of a lion's head on the chapel door – made c. 1373 in Romanesque style, probably to replicate the lost knocker of the church door at Stará Boleslav at which St Wenceslas was assassinated in 929 or 935.*

dimly lit hall on a square ground plan underneath a soaring canopy of the star vault upheld by massive ribs. The chapel protected the shrine of St Wenceslas, made of pure gold and gemstones (1358) and the saint's gold head reliquary. On it rested the

▲ *Statue of St Wenceslas – with the Parlerian Master's shield at its base, aleurolite, h. 200 cm. Designed and probably also carved by Peter Parler c. 1372, painted in 1373, restored in 1866. A contemporary wall painting of angels flanking the statue was renewed in the 1470s, probably for the coronation of Wladislaw II Jagiello.*
▶ *The chapel of St Wenceslas, eastward view. On the right the tomb of St Wenceslas, on the left the altar of St John, wall painting of the Crucifixion (after 1370, Master Oswald) and the statue of St Wenceslas; above, the portraits of King Wladislaw Jagiello and his wife Anne de Foix-Candale by the Master of the Litoměřice (Leitmeritz) Altar, c. 1515–16. The walls were encrusted with polished gemstones in 1372–73.*

St Wenceslas Crown of the Czech kings. The chapel was conceived in the image of New Jerusalem, no doubt by Charles IV, whose devotion to the saint was so deep that he had even written his own version of the legend of St Wenceslas. The lower walls of the chapel were inlaid by Parler's stonemasons with polished gemstones and embossed gilded stucco to frame the mural paintings of scenes of Christ's Passion by Master Oswald. On either side of the Crucifixion above the altar are depicted the Emperor Charles IV and his fourth wife Elizabeth of Pomorze (Pomerania). At the foot of the Cross is Prince, later King Wenceslas IV (1361–1419) and his wife Johanna of Bavaria. The best-known work in the chapel is the statue of St Wenceslas, designed, perhaps as early as the 1360s, and probably carved by Peter Parler for a tabernacle above the chapel, to direct pilgrims to the saint's grave. In 1372 or earlier Charles IV had it mounted instead above the main altar in the chapel. Paintings

▲ *Adam and Eve – the Original Sin depicted on the console of the south-eastern pier of the apse behind the main altar, before 1385. A statue of the Virgin stood once on this console. Parlerian sculptures of the 1480s anticipated the Beautiful Style, the Czech variant of the widespread "International Gothic".*

(pre-1509) higher up on the walls depict episodes from the legend of St Wenceslas, King Wladislaw Jagiello and Queen Anne de Foix-Candale.

Parlerian Sculpture

The renowned sculptures of the Luxembourg era in the cathedral were made from the late 1360s onwards. They are the work of Peter Parler and several talented stonemasons of his lodge, often his relatives, such as nephew Henry of Gmünd (to become parler of the lodge, later active in Brno and in Cologne, in the past mis-identified as Henry Parler, thought by some to have carved the statue of St Wenceslas), Hermann, Michael of Savoy, and Peter's sons Wenzel and Johann Parler.

The placing of the sculptures corresponds to the three-level symbolism of the cathedral. The tombs of ancient Přemyslid princes and kings rest on the ill-lit ground floor. The luminous triforium contains busts of Charles IV and his family and contemporaries of importance to the cathedral. Outside the church, beside the large windows of the high choir closest to heaven, are representations of Christ, the Virgin Mary and the patron saints of Bohemia. The flying buttresses and the roof bear numerous examples of medieval demonic imagery. Last came the sculptural decoration of the main tower, executed under Johann Parler.

Parlerian sculpture led to the emergence of the Beautiful Style.

◀ *Detail of the tomb of Czech king Přemysl Otakar II (1230–1278).*
▶ *Detail of the tomb of Czech king Přemysl Otakar I (c. 1155–1230).*
▼ *Tomb of Přemysl Otakar I, chapel of the Holy Relics, slate. This monumental tomb is one of the most important works of 14th century sculpture in Europe. In 1377 Peter Parler was rewarded for it by the Emperor with an exceptional fee of 900 groschen.*

▲ Elizabeth Přemyslid (1290–1330) – sister of Wenceslas III, the last Czech king of the Přemyslid dynasty, first wife of John of Luxembourg, queen of Bohemia, mother of Charles IV.

▲ Blanche de Valois (1316–48), daughter of count Charles d'Anjou et Valois, step-sister of French king Philip VI, first wife of Charles IV, queen of Bohemia.

▲ Anna Palatine (1329–53), daughter of Rudolf II, the influential Count Palatine of the Rhine and Imperial Elector, second wife of Charles IV, queen of Bohemia.

◄ Anna of Swidnica (1339–62), daughter of duke Henry II, third wife of Charles IV, queen of Bohemia, Holy Roman empress.

▲ Wenceslas IV. (1361–1419), son of Charles IV a Anna of Swidnica, Czech king (crowned 1363), Holy Roman king (elected 1376, deposed 1400).

▸ John Henry (1322–75), son of John of Luxembourg, brother of Charles IV, duke of Carinthia and Tyrol (1335–41), from 1349 margrave of Moravia.

▸▸ Wenceslas of Luxembourg (1337–83), son of John of Luxembourg and his second wife Beatrix de Bourbon, step-brother of Charles IV, count, and since 1354 duke of Luxembourg, duke of Brabant and Limbourg, author of lyrical poetry, buried in the Belgian abbey Notre-Dame d'Orval.

▲ Elisabeth of Pomorze (c.1347–93), granddaughter of Polish king Casimir the Great, fourth wife of Charles IV, Czech queen, Holy Roman empress.

▲ Johanna of Bavaria (c.1361–86), daughter of duke Albrecht I of Wittelsbach, first wife of Wenceslas IV., queen of Bohemia

◄ Man dressed like a monk – eastern console of the north portal of the chapel of St Wenceslas. The part of a batwing left of the broken-off other figure points to St. Procopius (†1053), founder of the Sázava Benedictine monastery, who was said to have overcome the devil and harnessed him to a plough. His Greek name is linked to his stay in south-eastern Europe whence he brought Slav monks to Bohemia. Not before 1369.

▶ The devil tearing out Judas's tongue – western console of the north portal of the chapel of St Wenceslas. According to the famous Golden Legend, having kissed Jesus, Judas was unable to give up his soul through his mouth. Not before 1369.

▼ Two large zoomorphic monsters in the corners below the cornice above the gallery of the great tower, c. 120 cm wide, probably by Johann Parler, before 1404.

Mascaron, male head with a large nose and bird's wings – outer tri-forium, Peter Parler's lodge, c. 1375.

Vegetable mascaron, console of a flying buttress supporting the high choir – Peter Parler's lodge, before 1385.

The mythical bird phoenix in flames, symbol of Christ and resurrection, outer triforium, Peter Parler's lodge, c. 1375.

▲ Christ before Pilate – *the chapel of St Wenceslas, one of a cycle of paintings of the Passion (the following scene, Christ at the column, is next to the candelabrum on p. 36),* *probably the work of court painter Master Oswald, buried in the cathedral (his tombstone is in the Lapidarium, the sculpture collection of the National Museum in Prague), 1372-3.*

▶ Adoration of the Kings, *chapel of SS. Adalbert and Dorothy ("Saxon"), wall painting by a follower of Master Theodoric, after 1376.*

Paintings of the Gothic Period

Little has survived in St Vitus's Cathedral of the original mural paintings. Fragments of murals from the reign of Charles are in the chapel of St Mary Magdalene – depicting the Virgin with saints and canons – and in the chapel of SS. Simon and Jude, showing the Madonna with saints. The paintings deserving particular attention are those attributed to the court painter Master Oswald, who is buried in the cathedral.

Apart from the *Cycle of the Passion* in the Chapel of St Wenceslas, he painted the *Man of Sorrows* and the *Beheading of St Catherine* on the western wall of the chapel of St John of Nepomuk and the *Miraculous Baptism of St Odilia* (who recovered her sight) on the eastern wall of the chapel. The donor was Archbishop Očko (†1380). In the same chapel is his marble tomb with three coats-of-arms painted on the wall above: the insignia of his offices of papal legate,

▸ *The* Miraculous Baptism of St Odilia *who thereby gained sight – wall painting, chapel of SS. Erhard and Odilia (opposite the altar tomb of St John of Nepomuk), Master Oswald, before 1378. At the font kneels the donor, second archbishop of Prague Jan Očko, himself partly blind.*

▲ St Vitus Madonna, *in its original carved gilded frame with medallions of angels, saints and the donor. Depicted are, from above, in pairs, SS. John Baptist and John Apostle, SS. Wenceslas and Vitus, SS. Sigismund and Adalbert (Vojtěch), archbishop John of Jenštejn and St Procopius, before 1396.*

This is one of the most outstanding works of the Czech Beautiful Style. National Gallery in Prague, Collection of Medieval art in the Convent of St Agnes of Bohemia.

▶ *Detail – St Wenceslas, painted relief on the gilded frame of the* St Vitus Madonna.

▲ The St Vitus Veraikon
(the true likeness of the Saviour) –
by an unknown painter, after 1400,
part of the cathedral treasure.
On the frame are painted images of
six Czech patron saints, from above,
in pairs, SS. Vitus and Wenceslas,
SS. Adalbert (Vojtěch) and Procopius,
and SS. Ludmila and Sigismund.

archbishop of Prague and bishop of
Olomouc. Oswald and his assistants
also painted the coats-of-arms on the
external southern staircase of the
cathedral. The spirituality of Oswald's
painting probably influenced the most
important painter of the Luxembourg
period in Bohemia – the Master of the

Třeboň (Wittenberg) Altarpiece.
    Another painter of the reign of
Charles IV, a follower of Master
Theodoric, painted a luminous
Adoration of the Kings on the west
wall of the chapel of SS Adalbert and
Dorothy ("Saxon") donated by the
Dukes of Saxony.

The Cathedral Treasure

The Treasure of St Vitus's Cathedral is the oldest, most venerable and historically most important in the Czech Lands. Its beginnings date to the reign of St Wenceslas (†935), who had to submit to the German King Henry I the Fowler and received from him an arm of St Vitus. Wenceslas consecrated to this saint the new rotunda with four apses at Prague Castle.
The cathedral acquired further riches from Charles IV, the leading collector of relics in medieval Europe and connoisseur of precious stones and of goldsmiths' work. His many gifts to the cathedral treasure were supplemented by bequests from his wives, the queens of Bohemia, and from Church dignitaries. At the Emperor's wish and with the Pope's approval, priceless relics from Karlštejn Castle and St Vitus's Cathedral were placed

◀ *Two oliphants (ivory hunting horns) decorated with hunting scenes, 49 and 55.5 cm long, work of Siculo-Arab type, probably 11th century. In the Middle Ages linked with the legendary hero Roland.*
  A similar "horn of Charlemagne" is kept in Aachen cathedral treasury.
◀ *The French reliquary châsse contained the relics of several saints. Copper gilt plaques with champlevé enamel. 10 x 20 x 27.5 cm, Limoges, 12th century.*

▲ *The iron "St Wenceslas Helmet" of Nordic type may have been made locally in the 9th century, with a nose guard on a band which is probably of Viking origin. The figure, until recently believed to represent Christ, is now thought more likely to show the Nordic god Odinn, who hung for nine days and nights on the huge World Tree, Yggdrasil, so that he would gain wisdom. Linked by tradition with St Wenceslas, the helmet became one of the symbols of the Czech state. With the so-called St Wenceslas Coat of Mail and Sword it has always been a revered part of the cathedral treasure. H. 17 cm.*

▼ *Foot of the Jerusalem Candlestick in the chapel of St John Baptist, seized in 1158 by Czech knights in Milan in whose capture by Emperor Frederick Barbarossa they had taken part. It represents the Tree of Jesse (below left), father of king David and grandfather of Solomon (below), believed to be Jesus's ancestors. The co-existence of beasts and men was predicted by Isaiah. The candelabrum was thought to have been taken from Solomon's temple in Jerusalem. The foot was cast probably in the basin of the rivers Meuse (Maas) and Mosel c. 1150–58. The base dates from 1395, the stem from 1641.*

▾ Onyx ciborium in the form of a chalice for the Holy Communion of the sick, donated by Charles IV, with his shields, Czech and Imperial, and an inscribed dedication. Made in Venice, the chalice was adapted in Bohemia. H. 15.4 cm, 1350.

▾ Reliquary cross of Pope Urban V – gold, black enamel, gemstones, behind the crystal lens a part of Christ's loincloth, below is depicted the presentation of the cross to Charles IV in 1368. Height 31 cm (without the Baroque foot).

▾ Crystal jug, silver gilt, gemstones, h. 39.5 cm. Made in Venice in 11–12th century, the jug was adapted in Prague c. 1350 to hold a part of the supposed tablecloth from the Last Supper presented to Charles IV by king Louis of Hungary in 1348.

on public view every year in what is now Charles Square. This event was discontinued in the Hussite period when a large part of the cathedral treasure was lost. Its return at the end of the Middle Ages was due to Wladyslaw Jagiello. In the course of the Counter Reformation that followed the battle of the White Mountain in 1620 the cathedral treasure was greatly enlarged.

In 1645 the reliquaries from Karl-štejn Castle were added to it, and in 1782 purchases were made from the dissolved Benedictine convent of St George at Prague Castle. In more recent times the funerary insignia of Czech kings Rudolf of Habsburg (†1307) and Přemysl Otakar II (†1278) were transferred from their tombs in the cathedral (1870, 1976).

Certain works from the cathedral treasure have been loaned to the National Gallery in Prague.

▼ *Tower reliquary with the Parlers' shield on the foot. Donated to the cathedral by a member of the Parler family. Silver gilt, h. 35 cm, c. 1370.*
Reliquary (ostensorium) of St Urasius, silver gilt and a crystal casket, h. 44 cm, made in the 2nd half of 14th century.
Tower reliquary of St Catherine, silver gilt and a horizontal crystal cylinder casket, h. 45 cm, c. 1380.

▶ *Head reliquary of St Ludmila, silver gilt, h. 34 cm, c. 1350, from the former Benedictine convent of St George at Prague Castle.*
▶ *Reliquary of St George, silver gilt, h. 56 cm, base in the form of a chapel with Madonna and Child, St George, Christ the Judge and St Ludmila, c. 1350, from the dissolved Benedictine convent of St George at Prague Castle.*

29

The Chapter Library

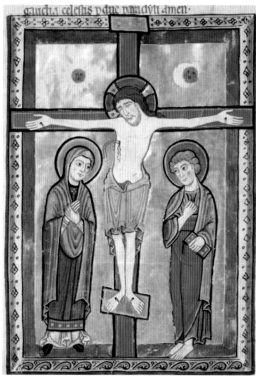

The Chapter library grew gradually inside the church as part of the cathedral treasure. Most valuable is its collection of 125 illuminated medieval and Renaissance manuscripts, e. g. a fragment of a 6th-century Gospel of St Mark with a long note written by Charles IV, Gospels written probably in the context of King Vratislav I's 1086 coronation, or an 11th century book containing the Apocalypse, the Acts of the Apostles and the Epistles of St Paul, the psalter *Codex ostroviensis* (c. 1200) and two copies of the influential treatise *De civitate Dei* (*The City of God*) by one of the Doctors of the Church, St Augustin of Hippo. Of the nine hymn-books, commissioned at great expense by the first

▲ *St John Apostle, St Vitus Gospels, late 11th century.*

▲ *Crucifixion – illumination in Byzantine style. Ostrov Psalter, c. 1200.*

▶ *The illuminator Hildebert, assistant Everwin and a mouse – copy of* De Civitate Dei, *before 1150. The drawing at the end of the manuscript is the oldest known genre picture in Bohemia. In the open book there is the curse – Pessime mus sepius me provocas ad iram ut te Deus perdat (Wretched mouse, you make me angry too often, God damn you).*

Archbishop, Ernest of Pardubice, six have survived. Most remarkable is the Missal of the Bishop of Olomouc John of Neumarkt (†1380). Wenceslas of Radeč, canon and fifth director of works (†1417), donated to the chapter an illuminated missal and a prayer book.

In 1552 the library received an antiphonal from the renowned workshop of Jan Táborský, lavishly illuminated by Fabian Puléř.

▲ *Heavenly Jerusalem in a later copy of the work* De Civitate Dei *by St Augustin of Hippo (†430), c. 1200. Below right a bishop, a monk, a man and a woman (prince and princess ?), identified as Boemienses (Czechs).*

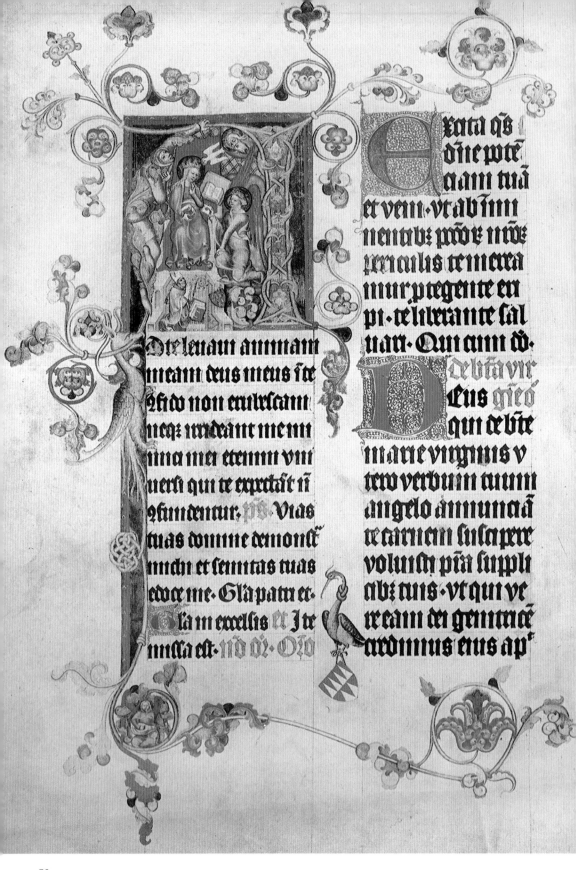

◀ The Annunciation. Initial A of the first verse of Psalm 25 ("Psalm of David"), Introit of the liturgy for the 1st Sunday of Advent ("Ad te levavi animam meam deus meus in te confido . . .") in the Missal of John of Neumarkt, bishop of Olomouc, chancellor and diplomat. Work of a court illuminator influenced by Italian art, after 1364. A sealed message from Heaven is formally presented to Virgin Mary by Archangel Gabriel. The arms of the Olomouc bishopric. are to the right of the donor.

▲ St Benedict teaching two Croatian Benedictine monks – illumination, Latin Bible from the Emmaus monastery in Prague, c. 1360.

▲ ▶ Pope (Boniface IX) on the throne of St Peter. Initial A, Missal of Canon Wenceslas of Radeč (director of works at St Vitus, see p. 7), c. 1400.

▶ The first archbishop of Prague Ernest of Pardubice praying to Christ, asking for guidance and help – illumination, Initial A of the plainsong setting of the first verse of Psalm 25 in the Gradual of Ernest of Pardubice, 1363. The supreme representative of the Church in the Czech lands and intimate friend of Emperor Charles IV has humbly laid aside the insignia of his office, "as if out of his love of God he treated them with disdain", according to his contemporary biographer.

Restoration of the Cathedral under King Wladislaw Jagiello

In 1485 King Wladislaw Jagiello (1456-1516) transferred the royal residence from the Old Town back to Prague Castle and began restoration work in the cathedral. To enhance the king's sovereign status the construction of a new Royal Oratory was begun by Hans Spiess from Frankfurt. It was completed after 1490 by Benedikt Ried (†1534), the architect of new castle fortifications, better known for the impressive Wladislaw Hall in the royal palace at Prague Castle, the largest secular hall of that time. Although he also made plans for the completion of the cathedral, only the foundations of the piers in the nave and of the north tower were laid. The chapel of St Wenceslas was refurbished, albeit not as lavishly as under Charles IV. Parler's statue of the saint (1373) was taken there and set among wall paintings of angels and

▼ *One of a pair of votive figures of miners holding lamps before the tomb of St John of Nepomuk. Painted and gilted wood, mid-18th century.*

▶ *Detail of the oratory balustrade – the double-tailed lion shield of Czech kings (first known use in 1197), today symbol of Czech statehood.*

Czech patron saints (1470s).

A cycle of scenes from the legend of St Wenceslas was painted on the upper walls of the chapel, allegedly for the 1509 coronation of Ladislav Jagiello. It dates more probably to the first Congress of Vienna of 1515 where the Emperor Maximilian and Wladislaw Jagiello agreed the rules of mutual succession of their descendants. In certain circumstances Ladislav might have become emperor. Such hopes were thwarted when in 1526 he died in the battle of Mohács. The main scene, above the western portal of the chapel, is of the miraculous arrival at an imperial diet of St Wenceslas, accompanied by angels, a reminder of the Czech ruler's senior

▼ *Royal oratory, Hans Spiess, 1493. On the balustrade the personal and land arms of Wladislaw Jagiello, King of Bohemia and Hungary.*

▶ *The miraculous arrival at the imperial diet of St Wenceslas – wall painting in the chapel of St Wenceslas, c. 1515–16. A symbolic reminder of the high status of Czech rulers in the Holy Roman Empire in the context of the unrealized aspirations of the Jagiellos for the imperial throne. The seat of the Czech elector is next to the emperor's throne – designated with Czech royal arms (double-tailed lion, this time without the crown which the king was dispensed from wearing at the emperor's court).*

status in the college of electors, disputed in the post-Hussite era.

On the wall opposite there are the portraits of Wladislaw Jagiello and his then already deceased wife Anne de Foix-Candale (†1506).

◀ Head reliquaries of St Adalbert (Vojtěch, †997), the first Czech bishop of Prague, and St Vitus, patron of Prague cathedral, whose relics St Wenceslas was said to have obtained following his miraculous reception at the legendary imperial diet. The bishop's mitre is decorated with gemstones. On the chest of St Vitus the relics are visible behind a lens-shaped crystal window. Silver gilt, h. 63 and 51 cm, late 15th century.

The second head reliquary in particular is an outstanding work of the goldsmith's art, showing signs of transition from Late Gothic to the Renaissance style.

These are two of the six head reliquaries commissioned for the cathedral by King Wladislaw Jagiello.

▼ The bronze effigy of Countess Ludmila of Thurn, née Berková of Dubá (†1558), governess of Emperor Ferdinand I's daughters, and her two sons – chapel of St John of Nepomuk. It is perhaps a late work of the Vischer foundry in Nuremberg.

◀ A monumental Renaissance bronze candelabrum with St Wenceslas under a canopy – donation of Old Town maltsters in memory of their predecessors who on 10 June 1421

forced iconoclasts out of the
cathedral. Cast in 1532 at the famous
Vischer foundry In Nuremberg.
In the north-eastern corner of the
chapel of St Wenceslas.

The wall painting of Christ at the
Column, one of the Cycle of the
Passion, is attributed to Master
Oswald. After 1370.

▲ The Assassination of St Wenceslas
– panel painting by Master I.W., the
most important follower of Lucas
Cranach the Elder in Bohemia, 1543,
completed by an assistant.

The Habsburg Accession

Elected King of Bohemia in 1526, Ferdinand I (†1564) was the founder of the Habsburg dynasty on the Czech throne (until 1918). Under his son Maximilian II (1564–76) royal architect Boniface Wolmut built the Mannerist music loft. Outside the temporary west façade the chapel of St Adalbert (later demolished, see pp. 63, 64) was built by his successor Ulrico Aostalli.

In 1566 Maximilian commissioned the royal mausoleum as a monument to the Habsburg monarchs and a tribute to their famous predecessors on the Czech throne. Modified by Rudolf II, the mausoleum was eventually completed in 1589.

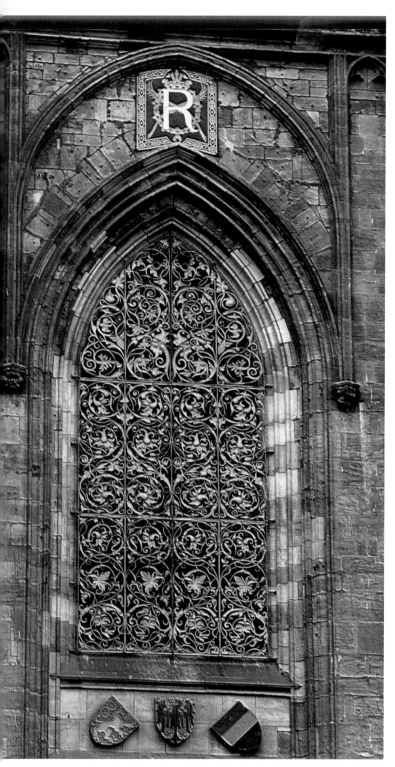

▲ The Post-Gothic net vault with skeletal 'flying' ribs in the ground floor chapel below the music loft. Boniface Wolmut, 1557–59.

▶ Music loft by Boniface Wolmut, 1557–59, Baroque parapet with reliefs of music instruments, 1729. The large organ was made by Anton Gärtner, 1763.

In 1924 the loft was transferred from the west side of the choir to the north side of the transept due to the merging of the medieval and modern parts of the cathedral.

▲ Gilded Renaissance grille of the lower belfry of the south tower by Georg Schmidthammer, 1568–73. Above is the monogram of Emperor Rudolf II, below the St Wenceslas eagle, the earliest Přemyslid arms, flanked by the Czech lion and the shield of the archbishopric of Prague.

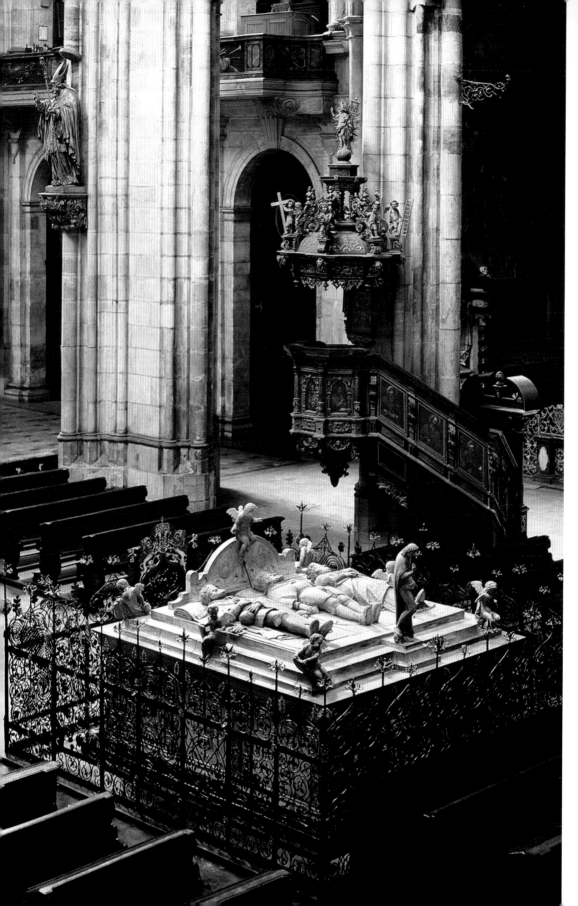

◄ Royal mausoleum – marble, gilding, by Alexander Colin's workshop, Innsbruck and Prague, 1566–89, grille by court locksmith Georg Schmidthammer, 1565, 1576–90. On top are the supine effigies of Ferdinand I, Anne Jagiello and Maximilian II, on the sides are medallions of Charles IV and his wives, Wenceslas IV, Ladislav Posthumous and George of Poděbrady. Behind is the early Baroque pulpit by Caspar Bechteler (1618), restored by him in 1630 and embellished with panels painted by Matthias Mayer. The Rocaille ornaments were added in the 18th century.

▲ Tin coffin of Rudolf II, 1612.
▼ Details of the mausoleum, from the left: Emperor Maximilan II, statue of the Saviour.
▼ Marble epitaph of Bernardino Menesto of Toledo (†1566), courtier of Ferdinand I, western wall of the southern wing of the transept.

The Defeat of the Reformation

On 23 May 1618 Czech Protestants threw imperial governors Slavata and Martinic from the windows of Prague Castle. This marked the beginning of the Thirty Years' War. In 1619 Frederick V Elector Palatine of the Rhine was elected King of Bohemia (1596–1632). His wife was Elizabeth Stuart, daughter of King James I.

The defeat of the army of the Czech Estates at the battle of the

◀ *Calvinists "cleansing" the cathedral of statues and pictures in 1619, part of a relief in the southern choir aisle, stained oak, by Caspar Bechteler, before 1630.*

▼ *Flight from the Castle of the "Winter King" Frederick Palatine, 1620, part of a relief, stained oak, by Caspar Bechteler, before 1630.*

White Mountain in 1620 led to the restoration of the rule of the Catholic Emperor Ferdinand II and to the onset of Counter-Reformation in the Czech Lands. Having been stripped of its decorations by Calvinists in 1619, St Vitus's Cathedral was re-consecrated in February 1621. The emperor replaced the lost retable with a triptych whose centrepiece was *St Luke Drawing a Portrait of the Virgin* by Jan Gossaert, called Mabuse (now in the National Gallery in Prague). The triptych was removed from the cathedral of St Rombold in Mechlin during its plunder in 1580 and taken from the Low Countries by the then Regent Matthias, Emperor Rudolf's brother and eventual successor.

Two events of the turbulent period are shown on the reliefs by court

cabinet-maker Caspar Bechteler on the back of the choir stalls – the iconoclastic "cleansing" of the cathedral by the Calvinists under Frederick the Palatine (1619–20) and the "Winter King's" flight from the Castle. He took the Crown Jewels with him, but in fear of pursuit he left them at the Old Town Hall. Two days later they were handed over to the victor. Bechteler made the pulpit which he had to restore and two elaborately carved cathedral doors (1630). They depict the Doctors of the Church, the evangelists and Bohemia's patron saints, including for the first time the future saint, John of Nepomuk. Before the demolition of the provisional west façade the doors were transferred to the chapel below the music loft.

Victorious Baroque

In 1673 Emperor Leopold I laid the foundation stone of a new nave to be built in Baroque style from designs by Giovanni Domenico Orsi, but in 1675 the work had to be abandoned because of lack of funds. A later project by Johann F. Schor was not realised (1729). The dynamic new style made a significant impact on the interior, but much has changed since then: the four silver busts of the Czech patron saints from the high altar, made in 1699 by Rinaldo Ranzoni to a design by František Preiss, are now in the Chapel of St John of Nepomuk. Eight Baroque statues of

▲ *Statue of St Vitus, one of a set of eight statues moved in modern times from the presbytery to the piers of the crossing – gilded wood, Franz Preiss, 1696.*
◀ *The altar of St Sigismund. Design by architect Josef E. Fischer von Erlach (?) executed in Prague by František M. Kaňka, sculptures by Franz I. Weiss, 1735–41.*
▶ *Tomb of the Supreme Chancellor of the Czech Kingdom Count Leopold Šlik (†1723). Design by F. M. Kaňka from a concept of Josef E. Fischer von Erlach, portrait bust by Matthias B. Braun, whose workshop produced the other sculptural decoration of the monument, 1724.*

the patron saints by the same Prague sculptor were moved from the presbytery to the piers of the crossing.

Of the Baroque altars, the boldly conceived retable of St Sigismund by Franz I. Weiss depicts the saint's apotheosis. Another work that has remained untouched is the silver tomb

▲ *The canopy of the tomb altar of St John of Nepomuk, carried by figures of flying angels, by goldsmith Ignác Novák, was erected in 1771.*

altar of St John of Nepomuk, one of the most important Baroque works in the country, erected on the original

▶ *Tomb altar of St John of Nepomuk (beatified 1721, canonised 1729) – patinated silver, designed by Josef E. Fischer von Erlach, wooden model by court sculptor Antonio Corradini, executed by Viennese goldsmith Johann J. Würth, completed in 1736. The red marble balustrade with sculptures of four Virtues 1746 is by Prague stonemason Josef Lauermann. The canopy carried by angels (1771) was made by Ignác Novák. Commissioned by Emperor Charles VI, the tomb of the famous saint of Czech Baroque was paid for from donations collected over several years.*

site of the patron saint's grave.

Glorified by Counter-Reformation, John of Nepomuk died in 1399 under torture ordered by Wenceslas IV in the context of his conflict with Archbishop John of Jenštejn. Mistakenly credited for refusing to reveal the secret of the confessional of the queen, he was canonised in 1729.

◀ *SS. Vitus and Cyril, detail of two of four silver busts on the altar of the chapel of St John of Nepomuk, made by goldsmith Rinaldo Ranzoni after models by Franz Preiss. Donated in 1699 by Archbishop J. Breuner.*

▲ The Baroque Old Provost's House and a granite obelisk (1928) on the site of an ancient Slav offering site.

▲ The Cathedral of St Vitus – southern façade in the third courtyard of Prague Castle. Situation since the completion of the church for the 1929 celebration of the Millennium of the martyrdom of St Wenceslas.

The Completion of the Cathedral

It was neither Jagiellonian Gothic nor Baroque, but the religious Romanticism of the early 19th century, with its nostalgic admiration for the golden age of Charles IV, that stimulated the completion of the Cathedral of St Vitus. The idea was first aired at the 1844 congress of German architects in Prague by Canon Václav Pešina, who was encouraged by the work on the cathedral in Cologne (since 1842). A Union to complete the cathedral was founded in 1859, and in 1862 building work began under architect Josef O. Kranner with the restoration of the medieval choir and the removal of much of its Baroque adornment.

Kranner restored the Crown Chamber above the St Wenceslas Chapel to accommodate the Crown Jewels on their return from Vienna to Prague after the Austro-Prussian War (1867). With the construction of the nave and aisles with side chapels, and the western façade with its towers, the former silhouette of Prague Castle

▶ *Pen drawing by V. Morstadt, 1826.*

▲ *Northern side of the transept (1896).*

was radically changed. From 1873 to 1898 the architect in charge was Josef Mocker, succeeded by Kamil Hilbert, who excavated the remnants of the two earlier churches. Conservationists fought in vain to preserve the enclosing wall between the old and new parts of the cathedral. The two parts were merged to very good effect. On 28 September 1929 – the year of the millennium celebrations of St Wenceslas – the completed cathedral was opened to the public.

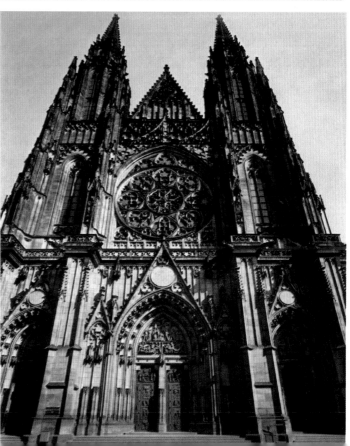

▶ *The Neo-Gothic west façade (1916).*

▲ Josef Kranner (†1871), first architect of modern works in the cathedral – bust by Jan Štursa, 1920.

▲ Josef Mocker (†1899), second architect of the completion of the cathedral – bust by Jan Štursa, 1920.

▲ Kamil Hilbert (†1933), third architect of the completion of the cathedral – bust by Bohumil Kafka, 1928.

▶ Central portal, western façade – in the tympanum are reliefs of the Crucifixion, Casting lots for Christ's garments and the Deposition, carved after World War II from 1939 designs by Karel Dvořák. The reliefs of scenes from the cathedral's history on the bronze doors, designed by Vratislav H. Brunner, were realised in 1926–29 by Otakar Španiel .

▲ Detail of the door– the translation of the relic of St Vitus to Prague; in the background the rotunda built by St Wenceslas on the present site of the chapel of St Wenceslas.

◀ The cathedral interior from the west – installed in the triforium are 14 busts of the leading personalities responsible for the completion.

Art of the Modern Age

The completion of the cathedral changed its aesthetic character and presented contemporary artists with challenging opportunities. The predominantly Gothic character of the chancel is the result of the policy adopted when Josef Kranner was in charge. He designed the Neo-Gothic high altar with a stone retable, completed in 1872 with some modifications by his successor Josef Mocker.

▼ *The monument of Archbishop Bedřich J. Schwarzenberg (†1885) – bronze, Josef V. Myslbek, 1891–95.*

Later the chancel was enriched with a unique monument by Josef V. Myslbek (1848–1922), the best Czech sculptor of his age, whose work inspired many followers. He created for Archbishop Schönborn a statue of his predecessor, Archbishop Bedřich Schwarzenberg. The confident treatment of the larger than lifesize, manly figure, and of the intricate draperies is reminiscent of the masterly funerary sculpture of 16th-century France (Germain Pilon).

Quite different is the impression of the altar by František Bilek, carved in 1896–9 (not consecrated), imbued

with mystic symbolism.

Decisions concerning decorations in the new parts of the cathedral were affected by the founding of the first Czechoslovak Republic (1918–38). A purely religious approach was complemented by the symbolism of the new state. Influential donors provided considerable financial support. The emphasis was on traditional aesthetics. Czech Modern art found expression in the austere adaptation of the royal crypt with new sargophagi, designed in 1935 by Kamil Roškot (1886–1945).

▲ ▶ The Altar of the Crucifixion with Virgin Mary in the northern nave – lime, oak and spruce, František Bílek, 1899, installed in 1927, one of the most important works of Czech fin-de-siècle symbolism, influenced by the ideas of the poet Julius Zeyer, with the inscriptions "My God, why hast thou forsaken me?" and "It is finished". The overall effect of this work of powerful spiritual subjectivism is that of an enduring "symbol of redemption, of triumph over pain and death".

The Stained Glass Windows

The prewar style was revived on the stained glass window in the New Archbishops' Chapel (1931) by the famous Art Nouveau painter Alphonse Mucha (1860–1939). Additional stained glass windows were commissioned from leading Bohemian glassmakers.

Interpretation of the subject matter was influenced by Josef Cibulka, a respected authority on ecclesiastical and art history.

František Kysela (1881–1941) of the School of Decorative Arts, designed in 1921 the large rose window of the west front on the subject of the *Creation of the World* (1928). His next

▲ The Creation of the World. *Rose window by František Kysela (1926).*

design for the Thun Chapel was on the theme of psalm 126, *He that soweth in tears shall reap in joy* (1934).

Other windows were designed by Kysela's former students and already

▲ Natural disasters, part of the window on *Psalm 126*, He that soweth in tears shall reap in joy *by František Kysela (1934). Thun chapel.*
▶ *Allegory of the* Beatitudes *from the design by František Kysela (1930–34) in the chapel of St Agnes of Bohemia.*

established artists, Cyril Bouda (1901–84) and Karel Svolinský (1896–1986).

The most important commissions were given to Max Švabinský, then a highly regarded professor at the Academy of Fine Arts. He created the windows in the chancel and the largest and most impressive stained

◀ Scenes with "the Apostles of the Slavs" from Thessaloniki, SS. Cyril and Methodius, the baptism of Prince Bořivoj, St Ludmila with young St Wenceslas. Painting on glass in the New Archbishops' chapel from a design by Alphonse Mucha, 1930.
▲ Window in the Schwarzenberg chapel by Karel Svolinský (1930–32), details with Abraham banishing Hagar and his son Ishmael and with the angel coming later to their rescue in the desert.

glass window in the south transept above the Golden Gate; his depiction of the *Last Judgment* is replete with references to Czech history, most appropriate in its position overlooking the traditional entrance of the coronation processions of the Czech kings.

▲ *Window in the Schwarzenberg chapel by Karel Svolinský (1930–32), details with Abraham preparing to sacrifice his son Isaac and the timely intervention by an angel.*
▶ *The* Corporal Acts of Mercy: *to feed the hungry, to give drink to the thirsty, to clothe the naked, to shelter the travellers, to free the imprisoned, to visit the sick, to bury the dead. Window designed by Karel Svolinský, 1931–33. In the chapel of the Holy Sepulchre.*

◀ The Descent of the Holy Ghost on the apostles with Virgin Mary. Window in the chapel of St Ludmila in the southern aisle. Each apostle's garment matches the colour of the gemstone symbolising his virtue. Design by Max Švabinský, 1933–35.

▶ The Holy Trinity, invoked by the Virgin Mary (adorned with the St Wenceslas Crown) and Czech intercessors (the Blessed Mlada, St Ludmila, St Wenceslas, St Vitus) with the founders of the earlier basilica and the cathedral (Prince Spytihněv II and Charles IV). The apse window was designed by Max Švabinský, 1946–48.

▲ Below the north window in the apse are depicted Elizabeth Přemyslid, mother of Charles IV, archbishop Ernest of Pardubice and Czech scholar canon Adalbert Ranconis de Ericinio, rector of the University of Paris.

▲ Below the south window in the apse are depicted Blanche de Valois, first wife of Charles IV, Archbishop John Očko of Vlašim and the great Czech theologian Thomas Štítný.

◀ The Last Judgment *in the southern arm of the transept. A new interpretation of the theme of the mosaic on the Golden Gate with Czech patron saints, kings buried in the royal crypt, the wives of Emperor Charles IV and other eminent Czechs, designed in 1935 by Max Švabinský.*

▶ *Scenes from the life of St Elizabeth and the martyrdom of St Barbara. Two details of the window in the southwestern entrance hall. From a design by Cyril Bouda, 1932.*

▼ *Laying the foundation stone of the nave of the cathedral on 29 October 1873 by Cardinal Bedřich Schwarzenberg in the presence of canons, politicians and other leading personalities. In front of the unfinished cathedral is the Baroque tomb chapel of St Adalbert (Vojtěch), demolished in 1879. The window in the Hasenburg chapel was made from a design by Cyril Bouda, 1933.*

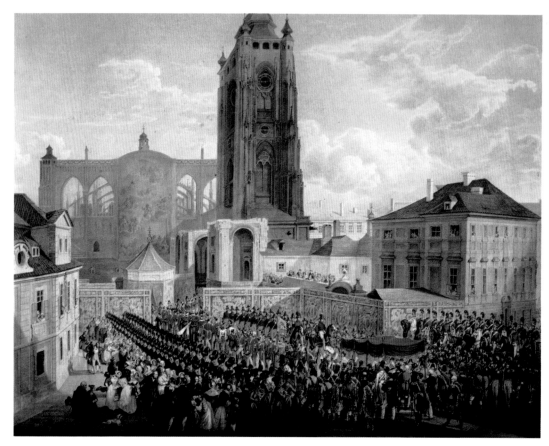

Historical Dates

1344 The foundation stone laid by King John of Luxembourg

1352 Death of Matthias of Arras, the first master-builder

1356 Arrival of Peter Parler, the second master-builder

1362 Completion of the sacristy

1367 Consecration of the chapel of St Wenceslas

1368 Consecration of the Golden Gate – *Porta aurea*

1370 Completion of the wreath of chapels and the aisles up to the level of the triforium

1371 Completion of the mosaic of the Last Judgment

1372 Completion of spiral staircase adjacent to the south transept

1373 Closure of the triumphal arch and the arches of the aisles

1376 Completion of the 11 windows of the high choir

1378 Death of Emperor Charles IV

1385 Consecration of the high choir

1396 Foundation of the south tower

1397 Wenzel Parler becomes the third master-builder

1398 Replaced by Johann Parler

1399 Death of Peter Parler

1406 Petrlik becomes master-builder

1419 Construction halted by Hussite uprising

1421 Cathedral decorations ravaged by Hussite iconoclasts

1437 Cathedral is re-consecrated

1490–3 Royal Oratory built by Hans Spiess and Benedikt Ried

1509 King Wladislaw Jagiello starts building work to complete the cathedral

1511 Construction halted due to lack of funds

1541 Fire causes heavy damage

1562 Great south tower completed in Renaissance style by Bonifaz Wolmut and Hans Tirol

1589 Royal Mausoleum completed by Alexander Colin

1619 Destruction of decorations by Calvinist iconoclasts

1621 Re-consecration of the church for Catholic worship

1673 Emperor Leopold I orders the construction to re-start in Baroque style. The work has to be halted due to lack of funds

1757 Bombardment by Friedrich II's Prussian army starts a fire

1771 Baroque adaptation of the

▲ *The cathedral before its completion, 1836. One of a set of twelve contemporary lithographs by Eduard Gurck, depicting the progress of the coronation as Czech king of Emperor Ferdinand V in 1836, the last such event to take place in Prague.*
On the western wall was a painting of the heavens with the Czech patron saints. In front of the provisional façade Ulrico Aostalli built in 1576 a chapel of St Adalbert (Vojtěch) above the saint's grave. That remarkable building was demolished in 1879.

main tower roof by N. Pacassi

1859 Union for the completion of the cathedral founded

1861 Architect Josef Kranner starts renovating the old church

1872 Main altar completed by new architect J. Mocker from Kranner's design with modifications

1873 Re-opening of restored church and start of new construction

1892 Completion of western towers

1899 Kamil Hilbert is third architect

1913 Chapel of St Wenceslas restored

1923–24 Dividing wall pulled down

1929 Consecration of the completed cathedral